# BATH BOMBS

Copyright © 2018 Laura K. Courtney

All Rights Reserved. No part of this book may be reproduced or used in any form or by any means without written permission from the author.

# TABLE OF CONTENTS

introduction .................................................................................. 6

What are Bath Bombs? ............................................................. 9

Bath Bomb Uses ........................................................................ 11

Ingredients and Equipment for Making Bath Bombs ........ 16

Storing Your Bath Bombs ........................................................ 21

Soothing Lavender Bombs ...................................................... 23

Calming Green Apple Bombs ................................................. 25

Citrus Crush Bath Bombs ....................................................... 28

Nourishing Gingerbread Bombs ............................................. 31

Herbal Bombs ............................................................................ 34

Lemon Vanilla Bombs .............................................................. 37

Therapeutic Bombs .................................................................. 40

Colds and Sinus Relief Bombs ............................................ 43

Fortifying Matcha Green Tea Bombs ................................ 46

Exotic Rose Bombs ............................................................. 49

Pain Relief Bombs .............................................................. 52

Pink Himalayan Salt Bombs ............................................... 55

Rejuvenating Coconut Oil Bombs ..................................... 58

Chamomile and Lavender Bombs .................................... 62

Rose Milk Bombs ................................................................ 65

Relaxing Grapefruits Bombs ............................................. 68

Detoxifying Bombs ............................................................. 71

Stimulating Oatmeal Bombs .............................................. 73

Regenerating Creamy Bombs ............................................ 76

Headache Relief Bombs.................................................................79

Meditation Bombs...........................................................................82

Healing Lavender Lemon Bombs .....................................85

Kids Calming Bombs ........................................................88

Bombs With Hidden Toys ...................................................91

Refreshing Aloe Bombs ....................................................97

Shea Butter Rosemary Bombs......................................... 100

Dandelion & Birch Oils Bombs........................................103

Healing After-Birth Herbal Bombs..................................106

Rosebud Bath Melts ....................................................... 110

White Chocolate Bath Melt............................................. 112

Moisture-Rich Milk & Honey Bath Melts ....................... 115

Other Books By The Author............................................. 118

# INTRODUCTION

Thank you for the purchase of *Bath Bombs: How to Make Beautiful and Nourishing Bath Bombs At Home, Using Cheap and Non-toxic Ingredients, Without Fuss*. This book provides you with everything you need to know about making your own beautiful and nourishing bath bombs without stress.

Have you ever had a refreshing bath using a bath bomb? Soaking in a bath with bath bombs can be a relaxing experience, especially if the bomb contains some bath salt and has a lovely scent. Have you ever wondered what makes bath bombs to fizzy once they touch water? That happens as a result of the chemical reaction that takes place between different ingredients used to create the bath bombs.

In this book, you'll learn how to make your own natural bath bombs that are chemical-free. You will also explore how modifying the ratio of different ingredients influences how much your bath bombs fizzy when you drop them in the bath. You'll be able to use creative methods to make some super satisfying bombs that suit your taste.

Bath bombs are a fairly easy project anyone can do - master crafter or novice. If you've failed to make bath bombs successfully in the past, try out my recipes and see if you will fall in love with fizzy making as much as I do. Whether you're making these super bombs for yourself, loved ones, or customers, these simple but gorgeous bath treat will help you relax your body and mind after a long day.

One of the amazing benefits of creating your own natural bath bombs is that you can easily tailor the ingredients to suit your specific needs. If you have any particular oil you prefer to use or you have an allergy you'll like to heal, you can make your own bath bombs to meet these needs. Making homemade bath bombs also save you time and money as well as helping you to make your own bath bombs for you and your family.

Thank you again for purchasing this book. I hope you enjoy it!

## WHAT ARE BATH BOMBS?

Bath bombs are a mix of fizzy ingredients, oils, salts, colorants, and some herbs or glitter, as the case may be. The sodium bicarbonate (baking soda) in bath bombs reacts with the citric acid to release carbon dioxide gas when they hit the water. This is similar to what takes place when you put an Alka-Seltzer tablet in a glass of water.

As this happens, the bath bomb begins to break apart, while releasing the skincare ingredients such as oils and salts, fragrances and colorants. This mixture changes your bath to a psychedelic blend of colors and scents that fill your entire bathroom. However, as far as your skin is concerned, there is no difference between adding salt and bath oils into your bath water. In other words, bath bombs allow you to add nourishing and moisturizing oils to your bath.

Although, some of the ingredients used can be irritating, especially dyes and fragrances. Not to mention picking glitter from sensitive areas. That is why it is important for you to learn how to make your own customized bath bombs to avoid irritation and allergies. This is less about function and more about the sensory experience.

## BATH BOMB USES

Bath bombs will keep their solid form as long as they're stored in a dry place. But, the fresher a bath bomb is, the more it'll fizzy when you add it to your bath water. Therefore, make sure you use up your bombs within a short period of time since they can lose some of their fizziness over time. However, the bombs will still smell wonderful and moisturize your skin.

There are many great ways you can use your bath bombs:

- **You may use a bath bomb to heal your skin condition.** If you have a skin condition like dry skin, sunburn, poison oak, poison ivy, dermatitis, acne, eczema, or any other skin ailment, you will probably find a bath bomb that will help you out.

- **You may use a bath bomb for sinus relief**. A bath bomb that contains eucalyptus oil will help you clear out your sinuses when you have a cold. All you need to do is to add a ball to warm bath water and hop in.

- **You may use a bath bomb for aromatherapy**. Bath bomb with essential oils can help to improve your mood and relax your mind, reducing stress and make you alert and focused. So when making your bath bombs, select the essential oils that suit your needs. Essential oils also help to give aroma to bath bombs. Here are some common essential oil for bath bombs and their uses:

    1. Peppermint essential oil has a cool, refreshing aroma that makes you feel energized and

refreshed. This oil also helps to ease headaches and nausea.

2. Lemon essential oil has a fresh, clean aroma that is uplifting, leaving you feeling energized and refreshed.

3. Rose essential oil has a classic aroma with sweet, floral notes. It helps to relieve depression.

4. Lavender essential oil has a great aroma with fresh, floral notes. This oil works effectively in reducing stress, anxiety, and depression.

- **You may use your bath bombs to create a luxury spa environment**. You can do this by playing some music, dimming the lights in your bathroom and lighting a few candles. Also, consider bringing some things that can make you comfortable since you'll be soaking for sometimes:

1. You can bring something to drink such as hot tea or champagne

2. You can bring something to eat like chocolate or fruit

3. You can relax with a book

4. You wear a facemask to the bathtub so that your face mask would have finished doing it work by the time you are done with your soaking.

5. You can fold a soft towel and place it behind your head or neck before you lean back in the bathtub to make things more comfortable for you.

- **You may use your bath bombs as an air freshener**. You can do this by displaying one or two bath bombs in a pretty dish in your bathroom. The bath bomb will release a subtle fragrance that is not overpowering.

- **Bath bomb-making can be a great DIY project for kids**. Some DIY beauty recipes such as homemade soap need accurate measuring and using harsh chemicals like lye make them too dangerous to make with children around. Making bath bombs is completely the opposite and is a fun project to do with a kid. Your kid can even think up of ways to mix colors, scents, and other customization.

# INGREDIENTS AND EQUIPMENT FOR MAKING BATH BOMBS

Bath bombs typically contain a wide range of ingredients such as bath salts, oils fragrances, food coloring and other components. However, there're a few key ingredients that most homemade natural bath bomb recipes contain: baking soda and citric acid. This is because when you mix baking soda with citric acid and place the mixture in water, a chemical reaction occurs. This chemical reaction creates lots of bubbles that you can see as the bath bomb dissolves in the water. The bubbles that cause the water to fizzy are made of carbon dioxide gas.

Another ingredient that is usually found in DIY bombs is cornstarch. The cornstarch acts as dry "filler" that you mix with the reactive citric acid and baking soda to make your bath bombs.

Most of the ingredients required to make bath bombs are pantry staples in many homes, however, ensure you have the following ready:

- **Citric acid**: This ingredient is responsible for the fizzling reaction of the bath bomb, which makes it feel like bathing in champagne. You can find natural citric acid in stores.

- **Baking soda**: This is the backbone of bath bomb making and it's an essential complement to citric acid and a part of the fizzling reaction. I recommend food-grade aluminum free baking soda.

- **Cornstarch or arrowroot**: This ingredient gives the bath bombs the silky feel we get from bath bombs. Organic cornstarch is great and you can also use arrowroot if you don't have cornstarch.

- **Salt**: You can decide to use basic salt, Epsom salt or any other salt of your choice.

- **Oils**: You may use simple oils like olive oil, coconut oil, almond oil, and apricot oil, all of which are great for a moisturizing bath.

- **Liquid**: Basic water works but you can use organic witch hazel for extra skin soothing.

- **Scents and colors**: Essential oils such as Lavender, Lemon, Rose, Eucalyptus, Rosemary, Peppermint, and Bergamot are great options for scents. You can also use dried herbs for scent and food coloring works well for colors.

Bath bombs are easy to make with measuring cups or bowls and your hands. However, it helps to have the following:

- A digital scale to get the right proportions

- Molds – you can easily mold your bath bombs into balls with your hands. But if you prefer fancier shapes or you're making them as gifts, molds are necessary. There are several packs of assorted shapes of molds available, including metal, plastic, and cupcake tins. You can also make use of muffin tray or ice cube tray

- Forks and spoons for mixing if you don't want to use your hand

- Medicine dropper

- Measuring spoons

Note that the recipes used in this book are meant for batching making. You can always make half or quarter of the recipes to your heart's desire. You may even double the recipe if you want, so have fun.

## STORING YOUR BATH BOMBS

Bath bombs need a very dry climate because moisture in the air can make your bath bombs to fizzy prematurely. A dry climate also helps while making the fizzies – creating bath bombs on a wet Pacific Northwest days can be a little complicated. So, if you live in a humid climate and make some bombs, a dehumidifier can help you preserve them.

Bath bombs, like most bath and beauty products, are often stored in the bathroom. Storing them in an airtight container will help protect the bombs from excess moisture. You can also wrap the bombs in plastic wrap to seal out moisture. The plastic wrap and jars also help to hold the crumbles that may fall off your bath bombs. These crumbles can be used for bath or used to make another bath bomb project. Always allow your bath bombs to dry completely before you wrap or package them.

Bath bombs will keep their solid form as long as they're stored in a dry place. But, the fresher a bath bomb is, the more it'll fizzy when you add it to your bath water. Therefore, make sure you use up your bath bombs within a short period of time since they can lose some of their fizziness over time. However, the bombs will still smell wonderful and moisturize your skin.

# SOOTHING LAVENDER BOMBS

This bath bomb recipe is very easy to make. They look pretty and smell wonderful. You will find them very relaxing. Enjoy!

## Ingredients

- 2 cups baking soda
- 1 cup cornstarch
- 1 cup citric acid
- 2 teaspoons purple soap colorant
- 50 drops lavender oil
- Witch hazel or water in a spray bottle

## Instructions

- Combine the dry ingredients in a large bowl.

- Mix up the remaining ingredients in a separate bowl and add to the dry ingredients. Mix well to combine.

- Make sure the mixture hold together when you squeeze a handful. If not, spritz lightly with witch hazel or water to achieve a damp consistency.

- Scoop the bath bomb mixture into molds and press firmly into the molds, place the two halves of the molds together.

- Leave them for 24 hours to harden before removing from molds.

- Drop one ball into your bath water just before you hop in and soak for about 30 minutes.

- Store the rest in an airtight container and place in cool dry place.

# CALMING GREEN APPLE BOMBS

These DIY bath bombs are great and have a charming scent you will enjoy while soaking in a warm bath. You can also give away some as gifts. This recipe will yield 6 big balls but you can reduce the recipe to your needs.

**Ingredients**

- 2 cups baking soda

- 1 cup cornstarch

- 1 citric acid

- 1 cup Epsom Salts

- 4 teaspoons apricot oil

- 4 teaspoons green apple essential oil

- Green food coloring

- Witch hazel or water in a spray bottle

**Instructions**

- Combine the dry ingredients in a large bowl.

- Mix up the remaining ingredients in a separate bowl and add to the dry ingredients. Mix well to combine.

- Make sure the mixture hold together when you squeeze a handful. If not, spritz lightly with witch hazel or water to achieve a damp consistency.

- Scoop the bath bomb mixture into molds and press firmly into the molds, place the two halves of the molds together.

- Leave them for 24 hours to harden before removing from molds.

- Drop one ball into your bath water just before you hop in and soak for about 30 minutes.

- Store the rest in an airtight container and place in cool dry place.

# CITRUS CRUSH BATH BOMBS

These citrus bath bombs are great and have a wonderful juicy scent from a generous amount of orange essential oil in the recipe. This recipe will give you about 6 big balls but you can always reduce it to the amount you want. Enjoy!

**Ingredients**

- 2 cups baking soda
- 1 cup cornstarch
- 1 cup citric acid
- ½ cup Epsom salt
- 4 teaspoons almond oil
- 1 teaspoon orange essential oil

- Orange food coloring

- Body glitter (optional)

- Witch hazel or water in a spray bottle

**Instructions**

- If you desire, spray some glitter in your molds and set aside.

- Combine the dry ingredients in a large bowl.

- Mix up the remaining ingredients in a separate bowl and add to the dry ingredients. Mix well to combine.

- Make sure the mixture hold together when you squeeze a handful. If not, spritz lightly with witch hazel or water to achieve a damp consistency.

- Scoop the bath bomb mixture into molds and press

firmly into the molds, place the two halves of the molds together.

- Leave them for 24 hours to harden before removing from molds.

- Drop one ball into your bath water just before you hop in and soak for about 30 minutes.

- Store the rest in an airtight container and place in cool dry place.

# NOURISHING GINGERBREAD BOMBS

These amazing bath bombs smell wonderfully sweet and fresh. They are a fun way of adding nourishing ingredients to your bath. Cinnamon, ginger, molasses and coconut oil used in this recipe all help to moisturize, hydrate and exfoliate the skin leaving you with a nourished, healthy skin.

**Ingredients**

- 1 cup baking soda

- ½ cup citric acid

- ½ cup Epsom salt

- 2 tablespoon coconut oil, melted

- 1 teaspoon molasses

- 1 teaspoon ground ginger

- 1 teaspoon cinnamon

- Witch hazel or water in a spray bottle

**Instructions**

- Combine the dry ingredients in a bowl and mix to combine.

- Add the molasses and melted coconut oil to the dry mixture. Mix until well combined.

- At this point, if you still need a bit more moisture to hold together, spritz witch hazel or water onto the moisture little by little until you reach the right consistency. However, be careful with water, you don't want to lose all the fizz before your bath.

- Scoop the bath bomb mixture into molds and press

firmly into the molds, place the two halves of the molds together.

- Leave them for 24 hours to harden before removing from molds.

- Drop one ball into your bath water just before you hop in and soak for about 30 minutes.

- Store the rest in an airtight container and place in cool dry place.

# HERBAL BOMBS

These homemade herbal bath bombs are relaxing and are especially great for before bed bath. Soak yourself and enjoy a nice, floral aromatherapy experience.

**Ingredients**

- 2 cups baking soda
- 1 cup citric acid
- 1 cup arrowroot powder
- 1 cup Epsom salts
- 5 teaspoons sweet almond oil
- 20 drops lavender essential oil
- 4 teaspoons dried chamomile flowers

- 4 teaspoons dried lavender flowers

- Witch hazel or water in a spray bottle

**Instructions**

- Combine the dry ingredients in a large bowl.

- Mix up the remaining ingredients in a separate bowl and add to the dry ingredients. Mix well to combine.

- Make sure the mixture hold together when you squeeze a handful. If not, spritz lightly with witch hazel or water to achieve a damp consistency.

- Place a pinch of the dried flowers on one side of the mold, cover with the bath bomb mixture until overfilled and press firmly into the molds; place the two halves of the molds together.

- Leave them for 24 hours to harden before removing

from molds.

- Drop one ball into your bath water just before you hop in and soak for about 30 minutes

- Store the rest in an airtight container and place in cool dry place.

# LEMON VANILLA BOMBS

These homemade bath bombs use vanilla and citrus which make it comforting and uplifting. This recipe will yield 6 bath bombs. Enjoy a lovely fizzy bath experience

**Ingredients**

- 2 cup s baking soda
- 1 cup cornstarch
- 1 cup citric acid
- 6 tbsp Epsom salts
- 6 tbsp dried lemon zest
- 1 tbsp melted coconut oil
- 1 tsp vanilla

- 30 drops lemon essential oil

- Witch hazel or water in a spray bottle

**Instructions**

- Combine the dry ingredients in a large bowl.

- Mix up the remaining ingredients in a separate bowl and add to the dry ingredients. Mix well to combine.

- Make sure the mixture hold together when you squeeze a handful. If not, spritz lightly with witch hazel or water to achieve a damp consistency.

- Scoop the bath bomb mixture into molds and press firmly into the molds, place the two halves of the molds together.

- Leave them for 24 hours to harden before removing from molds.

- Drop one ball into your bath water just before you hop in and soak for about 30 minutes.

- Store the rest in an airtight container and place in cool dry place.

# THERAPEUTIC BOMBS

These nourishing natural bath bombs are therapeutic. They are great for your skin and will give you an uplifting bath experience leaving you with a relaxed and nourished body as well as a happy and peaceful mind. Even though, most citrus essential are phototoxic, orange essential oil is not, which makes it great for bath bombs.

**Ingredients**

- 2 cups baking soda
- 1 cup cornstarch
- 1 cup citric acid
- ½ cup Epsom salt
- 4 tablespoons almond oil

- 1 teaspoon orange essential oil

- Orange food coloring

- Witch hazel or water in a spray bottle

**Instructions**

- Combine the dry ingredients in a large bowl.

- Mix up the remaining ingredients in a separate bowl and add to the dry ingredients. Mix well to combine.

- Make sure the mixture hold together when you squeeze a handful. If not, spritz lightly with witch hazel or water to achieve a damp consistency.

- Scoop the bath bomb mixture into molds and press firmly into the molds, place the two halves of the molds together.

- Leave them for 24 hours to harden before removing from molds.

- Drop one ball into your bath water just before you hop in and soak for about 30 minutes.

- Store the rest in an airtight container and place in cool dry place.

# COLDS AND SINUS RELIEF BOMBS

This amazing bath bombs help relief achy muscles and clear out sinuses simultaneously. They can be used just like typical bath bombs or placed in the shower to steam up and use it to clear out your sinuses if you don't want to have a bath.

**Ingredients**

- 2 cups baking soda
- 1 cup cornstarch
- 1 cup citric acid
- 6 tablespoons Epsom salt
- 2 tablespoons coconut oil
- 10 drops Eucalyptus essential oil

- 10 drops Peppermint essential oil

- Green food coloring

- Witch hazel or water in a spray bottle

**Instructions**

- Combine the dry ingredients in a large bowl and mix.

- Add coconut oil to the dry mixture and mix with your hand until the ingredients are well combined.

- Divide the mixture equally into two bowls. Add eucalyptus oil to one bowl and peppermint oil to the other bowl.

- Add green food coloring to the mixture that has eucalyptus essential oil.

- Lightly spray witch hazel or water into each bowl and

mix quickly until you have a damp consistency that can stick together when you squeeze the mixture in your hand.

- Layer your bath bombs molds with the different mixture to create fun stripe design. Or you can just fill up half of the mold with one color and the other half with the other color.

- Make sure you press tightly into the molds. Let them harden for about 24 hours.

- Gently remove from molds and store in an airtight container.

# FORTIFYING MATCHA GREEN TEA BOMBS

Matcha is everywhere these days. You can have it in your sauce, lattes, and smoothie and even in bath bombs. It's packed with nutrients and antioxidant which are great for the skin.

**Ingredients**

- 1 cup baking soda
- ½ cup cornstarch
- ½ cup citric acid
- 2 tablespoons rubbing alcohol
- 2 teaspoons Matcha powder

- 10-12 drops your ylang-ylang essential oil

- Witch hazel or water in a spray bottle

**Instructions**

- Combine the dry ingredients in a large bowl.

- Mix up the remaining ingredients in a separate bowl and add to the dry ingredients. Mix well to combine.

- Make sure the mixture hold together when you squeeze a handful. If not, spritz lightly with witch hazel or water to achieve a damp consistency.

- Place 6 tablespoons of the mixture into a separate bowl and set it aside.

- Add the matcha powder to the remaining bath bomb mixture in the first bowl and mix until combined.

- Fill one side of your mold with the matcha mixture until almost full, then layer with the white mixture. Press down firmly into the mold.

- Next, fill the other half of the mold with the matcha mixture until it is overflowing and press down tightly.

- Push the mold together to form a bath bomb and allow drying for 24 hours. Remove from molds, store in an airtight container and place in cool dry place.

- Drop one ball into your bath water just before you hop in and soak for about 30 minutes.

# EXOTIC ROSE BOMBS

These rose bath bombs are soothing and smell wonderful. This recipe uses dried rose hips which gives it a pretty pink color. It is so easy and cheap to make. And it will take you just 30 minutes to make.

**Ingredients**

- 2 cups baking soda
- 1 cup citric acid
- ½ cup kaolin clay
- ½ cup Celtic sea salt, fine grade
- 2 tablespoon rosehip seed oil
- 2 tablespoon rose hip extract or colorant (optional)

- 4 teaspoons sunflower lecithin

- 20 drops lavender essential oil

- 20 drops cedarwood essential oil

- 20 drops rose geranium essential oil

- Witch hazel or water in a spray bottle

**Instructions**

- Combine the dry ingredients in a large bowl.

- Mix up the remaining ingredients in a separate bowl and add to the dry ingredients. Mix well to combine.

- Make sure the mixture hold together when you squeeze a handful. If not, spritz lightly with witch hazel or water to achieve a damp consistency.

- Scoop the bath bomb mixture into molds and press

firmly into the molds, place the two halves of the molds together.

- Leave them for 24 hours to harden before removing from molds.

- Drop one ball into your bath water just before you hop in and soak for about 30 minutes.

- Store the rest in an airtight container and place in cool dry place.

# PAIN RELIEF BOMBS

This homemade bath bomb is far better than any commercial version. It's perfect for soothing and relaxing sore and aching muscles. It will also help to nourish your skin leaving you with a soft and smooth skin.

**Ingredients**

- 1 cup baking soda

- ⅔ cup Epsom salts

- 4 tablespoons melted coconut oil

- 4 tablespoons cream of tartar

- 1 teaspoon chopped fresh rosemary (optional)

- 2 teaspoons peppermint essential oil

- Witch hazel or water in a spray bottle

**Instructions**

- Combine the dry ingredients in a large bowl.

- Mix up the remaining ingredients in a separate bowl and add to the dry ingredients. Mix well to combine.

- Make sure the mixture hold together when you squeeze a handful. If not, spritz lightly with witch hazel or water to achieve a damp consistency.

- Scoop the bath bomb mixture into molds and press firmly into the molds, place the two halves of the molds together.

- Leave them for 24 hours to harden before removing from molds.

- Drop one ball into your bath water just before you

hop in and soak for about 30 minutes.

- Store the rest in an airtight container and place in cool dry place.

# PINK HIMALAYAN SALT BOMBS

This great recipe is very easy to make. It is perfect for a relaxed body and mind as well as a smooth and silky skin.

**Ingredients**

- 2 cups baking soda
- 1 cup citric acid
- 1 cup pink Himalayan salt
- 1 cup cornstarch, arrowroot
- 5 tablespoons almond oil
- 40-50 drops of any essential oil
- Witch hazel or water in a spray bottle

## Instructions

- Combine the dry ingredients in a large bowl.

- Mix up the remaining ingredients in a separate bowl and add to the dry ingredients. Mix well to combine.

- Make sure the mixture hold together when you squeeze a handful. If not, spritz lightly with witch hazel or water to achieve a damp consistency.

- Scoop the bath bomb mixture into molds and press firmly into the molds, place the two halves of the molds together.

- Leave them for 24 hours to harden before removing from molds.

- Drop one ball into your bath water just before you hop in and soak for about 30 minutes.

- Store the rest in an airtight container and place in cool dry place.

# REJUVENATING COCONUT OIL BOMBS

The coconut oil bath bombs are beautiful and very easy to make. The ingredients used in the recipes help to detoxify the body, relieve itchy and irritated skin, and moisturize the skin leaving you with a nourished and healthy skin. These amazing bath bombs are also great for soothing achy muscles.

**Ingredients**

- 2 cups baking soda
- 1 cup Epsom salt
- 1 cup cornstarch
- 1 cup citric acid

- 6 tbsp coconut oil, divided

- 2 tsp almond oil

- Vegetable-based food coloring

- Your favorite essential oil

- Witch hazel or water in a spray bottle

**Instructions**

- Add the dry ingredients to a large bowl and mix thoroughly.

- Divide equally into 3 bowls

- Mix two tablespoons of melted coconut oil and 4 to 6 drops of food coloring in a cup.

- Add 15 drops of essential oil and a ⅔ teaspoon of almond oil to the cup. Mix well to combine.

- Pour the coconut oil mixture into one of the bowls that have the dry ingredients and mix well with your hand. In case you'd like to add more color, mix the food coloring with melted coconut oil again and add to the bath bomb mixture.

- Repeat this process with different food coloring for the remaining two bowls.

- Scoop the mixtures into molds, layering different colors in each mold. Fill up the molds until overflowing. Make sure you press the bath bomb mixture firmly into the molds.

- Let the bath bombs dry for 24 hours. Remove from molds and store in an airtight container in a cool dry place.

- Drop one ball into a tub filled with warm water and

soak for 20 to 30 minutes.

# CHAMOMILE AND LAVENDER BOMBS

These homemade natural bath bombs are excellent for a relaxing soak in the tub. They are non-toxic and use natural ingredients that are great for soothing skin care. Enjoy!

**Ingredients**

- 2 cups baking soda
- 1 cup citric acid
- 4 tablespoons shea butter
- 2 tablespoons French green clay
- 1 tablespoon chamomile flowers
- 1 tablespoon colloidal oatmeal

- 1 tablespoon lavender essential oil

- ½ tablespoon lavender blossoms

- Witch hazel or water in a spray bottle

**Instructions**

- Combine the dry ingredients in a large bowl.

- Mix up the remaining ingredients in a separate bowl and add to the dry ingredients. Mix well to combine.

- Make sure the mixture hold together when you squeeze a handful. If not, spritz lightly with witch hazel or water to achieve a damp consistency.

-  Scoop the bath bomb mixture into molds and press firmly into the molds, place the two halves of the molds together.

- Leave them for 24 hours to harden before removing from molds.

- Drop one ball into your bath water just before you hop in and soak for about 30 minutes.

- Store the rest in an airtight container and place in cool dry place.

# ROSE MILK BOMBS

These lovely rose milk bath bombs help to turn your bath water to a spa-like sensuous milk color that leaves you with silky soft skin. This recipe is perfect for spoiling yourself and nourishing your skin.

**Ingredients**

- 2 cups baking soda

- 1 cup Epsom salts

- 1 cup citric acid

- 1 cup powdered milk

- 2 teaspoons almond or coconut oil

- 2 teaspoons lavender essential oil

- 2 teaspoons rose geranium essential oil

- Dried rose petals

- A few drops red food coloring for a soft pink color

- Witch hazel or water in a spray bottle

**Ingredients**

- Combine the dry ingredients, except the dried rose, into a large bowl.

- Mix up the remaining ingredients in a separate bowl and add to the dry ingredients. Mix well to combine.

- Make sure the mixture hold together when you squeeze a handful.

- Scoop the bath bomb mixture into molds and add a small pinch of the dried rose petal to one side of the mold, carefully cover them with the bath bombs mixture.

- Fill the molds until each side is overfilled and press firmly into the molds, place the two halves of the molds together.

- Leave them for 24 hours to harden before removing from molds.

- Drop one ball into your bath water just before you hop in and soak for about 30 minutes.

- Store the rest in an airtight container and place in cool dry place.

# RELAXING GRAPEFRUITS BOMBS

These amazing bath bombs smell delicious and they are so easy to make. You can enjoy a spa-like bath with this nourishing grapefruit bath bombs.

**Ingredients**

- 2 cups baking soda
- 1 cup citric acid
- 4 tbsp Epsom salt
- 6 tbsp melted coconut oil
- 20 drops grapefruit essential oil
- 6-10 drops food coloring
- Witch hazel or water in a spray bottle

## Instructions

- Combine the dry ingredients in a large bowl.

- Mix up the remaining ingredients in a separate bowl and add to the dry ingredients. Mix well to combine.

- Make sure the mixture hold together when you squeeze a handful. If not, spritz lightly with witch hazel or water to achieve a damp consistency.

- Scoop the bath bomb mixture into molds and press firmly into the molds, place the two halves of the molds together.

- Leave them for 24 hours to harden before removing from molds.

- Drop one ball into your bath water just before you hop in and soak for about 30 minutes.

- Store the rest in an airtight container and place in cool dry place.

# DETOXIFYING BOMBS

This wonderful recipe uses activated charcoal which is perfect for cleansing and detoxifying the skin leaving you with a smooth and soft skin.

## Ingredients

- 1½ cups baking soda
- ¾ citric acid
- 2 tbsp food-grade activated charcoal
- 6 tbsp melted coconut oil
- 15 drops of your favorite essential oil
- Witch hazel or water in a spray bottle

## Instructions

- Combine the dry ingredients in a large bowl.

- Mix up the remaining ingredients in a separate bowl and add to the dry ingredients. Mix well to combine.

- Make sure the mixture hold together when you squeeze a handful. If not, spritz lightly with witch hazel or water.

- Scoop the bath bomb mixture into molds and press firmly into the molds, place the two halves of the molds together.

- Leave them for 24 hours to harden before removing from molds.

- Drop one ball into your bath water just before you hop in and soak for about 30 minutes.

- Store the rest in an airtight container and place in cool dry place.

# STIMULATING OATMEAL BOMBS

These homemade lavender oatmeal bath bombs are easy to make and have a soothing effect on the skin. It helps to relieve dry and irritated skin as well as relaxing and calming the body.

**Ingredients**

- 2 cups baking soda

- 1 cup cornstarch

- 1 cup citric acid

- 1 cup quick cook oats

- ½ cup Epsom salts

- 3 tablespoons coconut oil, fractionated

- ½ teaspoon lavender essential oil

- Few drops purple gel food coloring

- Dried lavender flowers (optional)

- Witch hazel or water in a spray bottle

**Instructions**

- Combine the dry ingredients except for the dried lavender flowers in a large bowl.

- Mix up the remaining ingredients in a separate bowl and add to the dry ingredients. Mix well to combine.

- Make sure the mixture hold together when you squeeze a handful. If not, spritz lightly with witch hazel or water.

- Sprinkle a pinch of dried lavender flowers on one

side of the mold, cover with the bath bomb mixture until overfilled and press firmly into the molds, place the two halves of the molds together.

- Leave them for 24 hours to harden before removing from molds.

- Drop one ball into your bath water just before you hop in and soak for about 30 minutes.

- Store the rest in an airtight container or shrink bags and store in a cool dry place.

# REGENERATING CREAMY BOMBS

These lovely creamy bath bombs are great. They feel soothing and luxurious in the tub. Enjoy!

## Ingredients

- 2 cups baking soda
- 1 cup citric acid
- ¼ cup cocoa butter, melted
- 1 tablespoon oat extract
- 1 tablespoon colloidal oatmeal
- ½ tablespoon oatmeal milk and honey fragrance oil
- ½ tablespoon polysorbate 80
- Witch hazel or water in a spray bottle

## Instructions

- Combine the dry ingredients in a large bowl.

- Mix up the remaining ingredients in a separate bowl and add to the dry ingredients. Mix well to combine.

- Make sure the mixture hold together when you squeeze a handful. If not, spritz lightly with witch hazel or water.

- Sprinkle a pinch of oatmeal to the bottom of one half of the mold, cover with the bath bomb mixture until overfilled and press firmly into the molds, place the two halves of the molds together.

- Leave them for 24 hours to harden before removing from molds.

- Drop one ball into your bath water just before you hop in and soak for about 30 minutes.

- Store the rest in an airtight container or shrink bags and store in a cool dry place.

# HEADACHE RELIEF BOMBS

These easy DIY bath bombs work really well for soothing a headache and giving instant relief. The combination of peppermint and lavender essential oils make these bath bombs a natural headache remedy.

**Ingredients**

- 2 cups baking soda
- 1 cup Epsom salt
- 1 cup citric acid
- 1½ cup cornstarch
- 4 tbsp almond oil
- 2 tsp green mica powder

- 20 drops peppermint essential oil

- 20 drops lavender essential oil

- Witch hazel or water in a spray bottle

**Instructions**

- Combine the dry ingredients in a large bowl.

- Mix up the remaining ingredients in a separate bowl and add to the dry ingredients. Mix well to combine.

- Make sure the mixture hold together when you squeeze a handful. If not, spritz lightly with water to achieve a damp consistency.

-  Scoop the bath bomb mixture into molds and press firmly into the molds, place the two halves of the molds together.

- Leave them for 24 hours to harden before removing from molds.

- Drop one ball into your bath water just before you hop in and soak for about 30 minutes.

- Store the rest in an airtight container and place in cool dry place.

# MEDITATION BOMBS

This amazing bath bomb recipe is great for the body and mind. It's even better if you can add it to your bath at night, right before bed. Enjoy this treat and pamper yourself with a nice, floral aromatherapy experience.

**Ingredients**

- 2 cups baking soda //
- 1 cup cornstarch
- 1 cup citric acid
- 6 tablespoons Epsom salt
- 6 teaspoons coconut oil, unrefined
- 10 drops frankincense essential oil

- 10 drops cedarwood essential oil

- 8 drops sweet orange essential oil

- 8 drops lavender essential oil

- 4 drops ylang-ylang essential oil

- Orange mica powder (optional)

- Witch hazel or water in a spray bottle

**Instructions**

- Combine the dry ingredients in a large bowl.

- Mix up the remaining ingredients in a separate bowl and add to the dry ingredients. Mix well to combine.

- Make sure the mixture hold together when you squeeze a handful. If not, spritz lightly with water to achieve a damp consistency.

- Scoop the bath bomb mixture into molds and press firmly into the molds, place the two halves of the molds together.

- Leave them for 24 hours to harden before removing from molds.

- Drop one ball into your bath water just before you hop in and soak for about 30 minutes.

- Store the rest in an airtight container and place in cool dry place.

# HEALING LAVENDER LEMON BOMBS

These homemade lavender lemon bath bombs are excellent for relieving allergies. These soothing bath bombs have a great aroma and you can enjoy them anytime even without allergies.

**Ingredients**

- 2 cups baking soda
- 1 cup cornstarch
- 1 cup citric acid
- 6 tablespoons Epsom salt
- 2 tablespoons coconut oil
- 10 drops lavender essential oil

- 10 drops lemon essential oil

- Food coloring (your preferred colors)

- Spritz of witch hazel or water

**Instructions**

- Combine the dry ingredients in a large bowl and mix.

- Add coconut oil to the dry mixture and mix with your hand until the ingredients are well combined

- Divide the mixture equally into two bowls. Add lavender essential oil to one bowl and lemon essential oil to the other bowl.

- Add about 8 drops of food coloring to each bowl and mix well to combine.

- Lightly spray witch hazel or water into each bowl and

mix quickly until you have a damp consistency that can stick together when you squeeze the mixture in your hand.

- Layer your bath bombs molds with the different mixture to create fun stripe design. Or you can just fill up half of the mold with one color and the other half with the other color.

- Make sure you press tightly into the molds. Place the two halves of the molds together.

- Let them harden for about 24 hours.

- Gently remove from molds and store in an airtight container.

- For the bath, drop one ball into your bath water just before you hop in and soak for about 30 minutes.

# KIDS CALMING BOMBS

This great bath bomb recipe is safe for kids. You can give your child a relaxing bath at bedtime or use it to calm an anxious child. Chamomile and lavender essential oils used in this recipe help to soothe and calm an anxious nerve. These bath bombs also smell wonderful.

**Ingredients**

- ½ cup baking soda
- 1 cup citric acid
- 1 cup cornstarch
- 1 cup Epsom salt
- 2 teaspoons melted coconut oil
- 15 drops chamomile essential oil

- 15 drops lavender essential oil

- 15 drops vetiver essential oil

- Blue soap colorant (optional)

- Spritz of witch hazel or water

**Instructions**

- Combine the dry ingredients in a large bowl.

- Mix up the remaining ingredients in a separate bowl and add to the dry ingredients. Mix well to combine.

- Make sure the mixture hold together when you squeeze a handful. If not, spritz lightly with water to achieve a damp consistency.

- Scoop the bath bomb mixture into molds and press firmly into the molds, place the two halves of the molds together.

- Leave them for 24 hours to harden before removing from molds.

- Drop two balls into warm bath water and let your little one soak in it for about 15 -20 minutes.

- Store the rest in an airtight container and place in cool dry place.

# BOMBS WITH HIDDEN TOYS

Make handmade bath bombs for your kids to make bath time fun. With this recipe, you can hide any nice toy in the bombs to give your kid a pleasant surprise. You can also make an amazing handmade gift for birthdays, Mother's Day, Christmas and other occasions. This is also a fun craft project to make with kids. Have fun!

**Ingredients for bath bomb base**

- 2 cups baking soda
- 1 cup cornstarch
- 1 cup Epsom salts
- 1 cup citric acid

## Bath bomb fragrances options

You can choose any of the following colors and scents for your bath bombs. The color and scent you add to the base are where the creativity and fun come into play.

1. **Sweet citrus scent**

This sweet bath bomb scent will give you drool-worthy aroma leaving the kids energized and smelling good.

## Ingredients

- 8 tbsp coconut oil

- drops of pink food coloring (depending on your preferred intensity)

- 20 drops vanilla essential oil

- 20 drops grapefruit bergamot essential oil blend (or any other citrus essential oil)

## 2. Green cold fighting bath bomb scent

This bath bomb scent uses eucalyptus and peppermint essential oils which makes it perfect for congested chests and stuffy nose.

**Ingredients**

- 8 tbsp coconut oil
- drops of green food coloring
- 20 drops peppermint essential oil
- 20 drops eucalyptus essential oil

## 3. Sleepy-time lavender scent

This amazing bath bombs will send your little ones off to dreamland with the soothing aroma of vanilla and lavender essential oils.

**Ingredients**

- 8 tbsp coconut oil

- drops of purple, red, or blue food coloring (depending on your preferred intensity)

- 20 drops vanilla essential oil

- 20 drops lavender essential oil

**You'll also need:**

- Witch Hazel or water in a spray bottle, to add moisture if needed.

- Shopkins, action figure or any other small toy

- Molds such as meatball tongs, plastic Easter eggs, plastic Christmas ornaments, plastic bath bomb molds, metal bath bomb molds, , or soap molds.

**Instructions**

- Combine the bath bomb base ingredients in a large bowl and mix well.

- Choose a scent for your bath bombs and add the scent ingredients to a microwave-safe bowl. Microwave until coconut oil is melted (about 30 – 60 seconds)

- Add the melted bath bomb scent ingredients to the dry ingredients. Mix well to combine.

- Make sure the mixture hold together when you

squeeze a handful. If not, spritz lightly with witch hazel or water.

- Pack the mixture into the bath bomb mold and make it half full. Place the toy in the center and add more bath bomb mixture until overfilled. Place the two halves of the bath bomb molds tightly together.

- Gently open the mold and remove the bath bomb, if it starts to crack, turn it sideways and re-pack the bath bomb mixture into the mold; this will prevent bath bombs from cracking.

- After you have removed the bath bombs from molds, lay them out to dry for 24 hours. Then, store in an airtight bag or container.

- To use, drop one in the bath and let your little one soak for 15 to 20 minutes.

# REFRESHING ALOE BOMBS

This herbal bath bomb recipe is soothing and smells nice. The bath bombs are so easy to make and you can present as gifts to loved ones.

**Ingredients**

- 2 cups baking soda

- 1 cup citric acid

- 1 cup arrowroot powder or cornstarch

- ½ cup Epsom salts

- 2 tea bag of Earl Grey

- 5 teaspoons sweet almond oil

- 2 teaspoons aloe vera juice (place it in a spray bottle)

- 20 drops of chamomile essential oil

- 4 teaspoons dried chamomile flowers

**Instructions**

- Combine the dry ingredients, except dried chamomile, in a large bowl.

- Mix up the oils in a separate bowl and add to the dry ingredients. Mix well to combine.

- Spray the mixture with aloe vera juice while mixing with your until you achieve a damp consistency.

- Make sure the mixture hold together when you squeeze a handful. If not, spritz slightly with the aloe vera juice.

- Sprinkle a pinch of dried chamomile on one side of the mold, cover with the bath bomb mixture until overfilled and press firmly into the molds, place the two halves of the molds together.

- Leave them for 24 hours to harden before removing from molds.

- Drop one ball into your bath water just before you hop in and soak for about 30 minutes.

- Store the rest in an airtight container or shrink bags and store in a cool dry place.

# SHEA BUTTER ROSEMARY BOMBS

These rosemary shea butter bath bombs are awesome. They are soothing and relaxing for the body and mind. Make this amazing recipe at home for a spa-like experience.

**Ingredients**

- 2 cups baking soda

- 1 cup citric acid

- 1 cup arrowroot powder or cornstarch

- 8 tablespoons shea butter, melted

- 20 drops rosemary essential oil

- 4 teaspoons dried rosemary

- Witch hazel or water in a spray bottle

## Instructions

- Combine the dry ingredients in a large bowl.

- Mix up the remaining ingredients in a separate bowl and add to the dry ingredients. Mix well to combine.

- Make sure the mixture hold together when you squeeze a handful. If not, spritz lightly with witch hazel or water to achieve a damp consistency.

- Place a pinch of dried rosemary on one side of the mold, cover with the bath bomb mixture until overfilled and press firmly into the molds; place the two halves of the molds together.

- Leave them for 24 hours to harden before removing from molds.

- Drop one ball into your bath water just before you hop in and soak for about 30 minutes

- Store the rest in an airtight container and place in cool dry place.

# DANDELION & BIRCH OILS BOMBS

This herbal bath bomb recipe helps to soothe sore muscles with the combination of birch and dandelion infused oils and Epsom salts.

**Ingredients**

- 2 cups baking soda
- ½ cup Epsom salt
- 1 cup citric acid
- 1 tbsp birch infused oil
- 1 tbsp dandelion infused oil
- 2 tsp Matcha powder (optional)
- 25 drops energize essential oil blend or any other you

prefer

- Spritz of Witch hazel or water

## Instructions

- Combine the dry ingredients in a large bowl.

- Mix up the remaining ingredients in a separate bowl and add to the dry ingredients. Mix well to combine.

- Make sure the mixture hold together when you squeeze a handful. If not, spritz lightly with witch hazel or water.

- Scoop the bath bomb mixture into molds and press firmly into the molds, place the two halves of the molds together.

- Leave them for 24 hours to harden before removing from molds.

- Drop one ball into your bath water just before you hop in and soak for about 30 minutes.

- Store the rest in an airtight container and place in cool dry place.

# HEALING AFTER-BIRTH HERBAL BOMBS

This amazing bath fizzies are great for a new mom due to its soothing and healing properties. After giving birth, a new mom needs all the help she can get including a soothing bath. This recipe contains natural herbs and ingredients without harsh artificial colors and fragrances that could irritate tender postpartum areas.

**Ingredients**

- 2 cups baking soda
- 1 cup Epsom salt
- 1 cup citric acid
- 4 tsp olive oil

- 2 tsp vanilla extract

- Few drops of essential oil (optional)

- Witch hazel or water in a spray bottle

- 1 cup finely ground after-birth dried herbs (grind in a blender or food processor)

**After-birth dried herbs ingredients:**

- ½ cup red raspberry leaf

- ½ cup lavender flowers

- ¼ cup uva ursi leaf

- ¼ cup shepherd's purse

- ¼ cup calendula flowers

- ¼ cup yarrow flower

- ¼ cup plantain leaf

- ¼ cup comfrey leaf

Mix the herbs in a plaster bag or glass container and store up to a year in a cool dark place.

## Instructions

- Mix baking soda, citric acid and Epsom salt in a bowl.

- In a small bowl, mix witch hazel or water, vanilla extract, olive oil and essential oil if you're using, and then add the mixture to the dry mixture and mix very well.

- Add the finely ground herbs and mix until combined.

- Make sure the mixture hold together when you squeeze a handful. If not, spritz lightly with witch hazel or water.

- Scoop the bath bomb mixture into molds and press firmly into the molds, place the two halves of the molds together.

- Leave them for 24 hours to harden before removing from molds.

- Drop one ball into your bath water just before you hop in and soak for about 30 minutes.

- Store the rest in an airtight container and place in cool dry place.

# ROSEBUD BATH MELTS

This gorgeous sweet smelling bath melts give you the feeling of love and romance. This luxurious skin-moisturizing melts will leave your skin smooth and fresh.

**Ingredients**

- 1 ½ cups shea butter

- 1 ½ cups cocoa butter

- 2 tbsp coconut oil

- 20 drops orange essential oil

- 20 drops bergamot essential oil

- 30 drops joy young living essential oil

- Dried mini-rosebuds, food-grade (optional)

- Molds or an ice cube tray

**Instructions**

- Melt the coconut oil, shea butter, and cocoa butter.

- Add essential oils and stir to combine.

- Add dried rosebuds to the cavity of each mold if desired. Pour mixture into molds or an ice cube tray.

- Place in the refrigerator for a few hour to set. Gently remove from molds and store in a cool dry place.

- To use, drop one or two of the bath melts in a warm bath water, add a cup of Epsom salt to your bath if you want and soak for 30 minutes.

**Note**: The bath will be slippery because of the bath melts so be careful. You may use a good quality bath mat to avoid slipping. Make sure you wipe the bath clean after use.

# WHITE CHOCOLATE BATH MELT

Indulge yourself in the chocolate-scented moisturizing bath treats. They're so simple to make and blend better with fragrances. These bath melts will leave your skin looking and feeling smooth and silky. Using unrefined cocoa butter will give you a stronger smell of chocolate.

## Ingredients

- 50g white cocoa butter

- 25ml coconut oil

- 10 drops lavender, peppermint, sweet orange, or rose essential oil

- Chocolate molds or an ice cube tray

## Instructions

- Cut your cocoa butter into small pieces with a sharp knife or simply grate the butter.

- Boil about 1½ cup of water in a saucepan and allowing simmering to a low temperature.

- Place the coconut oil and cocoa butter in a small bowl and place the bowl over the saucepan to melt the butter.

- Once the butter is melted, remove from heat and add the essential oil and mix.

- Pour mixture into molds or an ice cube tray.

- Place in the refrigerator for a few hour to set. Gently remove from molds and store in a cool dry place.

- To use, drop one or two of the bath melts in a warm bath water, add a cup of Epsom salt to your bath if you want and soak for 30 minutes.

**Note**: The bath will be slippery because of the bath melts so be careful. You may use a good quality bath mat to avoid slipping. Make sure you wipe the bath clean after use.

# MOISTURE-RICH MILK & HONEY BATH MELTS

This homemade natural bath melt helps to soothe dry, itchy skin while you soak away. It contains all natural non-toxic ingredients like mango or shea butter, honey, milk and almond oil. It also helps to exfoliate the skin getting rid of dead skin cells and leaving you with soft and smooth skin.

**Ingredients**

- 2 cups milk, powdered
- 1½ cups honey
- ⅔ cup mango butter or shea butter
- ⅔ cup almond oil

- 1 cup milk, powdered (for rolling)

## Instructions

- Add the mango butter or shea butter, honey and almond oil to a heat-resistant bowl.

- Place the bowl into a saucepan filled with boiling water to melt the butter.

- Remove from the boiling water and stir in the powdered milk.

- Roll two tablespoons of your mixture into a tight ball. Repeat the process for the rest of the mixture.

- Place the rolled mixture on a parchment paper or wax paper and allow cooling.

- Roll the bath melts in 1 cup of powdered milk for a decorative finish.

- To use, simply fill your tub with hot water. Drop one or two bath melts in to melt. Soak for 20 – 30 minutes, and then rinse your body with clean water.

**Note**: The bath will be slippery because of the bath melts so be careful. You may use a good quality bath mat to avoid slipping. Make sure you wipe the bath clean after use.

# OTHER BOOKS BY THE AUTHOR

1. All Natural Soap Making

2. Natural Healing with Essential Oils

3. Hair Care and Hair Growth Secrets

4. Clean Your Home with 66 Homemade Cleaning Products

5. Epsom Salt, Apple Cider Vinegar and Honey Natural Remedies

Printed in Great Britain
by Amazon